© HAPPINESS MAGNET
BY SANDEEP RAVIDUTT SHARMA

Table of Contents

Introduction IV

Happiness Magnet..1

© HAPPINESS MAGNET
BY SANDEEP RAVIDUTT SHARMA

Introduction

This book provides you with a list of **100 motivational quotes and thoughts** focussing mainly on improving your wellness quotient. You need to start somewhere if you have planned your destination. Don't expect to run right from the first step. Build the momentum gradually and you can reach your destination in time. Success awaits you if you take the right step forward full of self-belief and determination. **Become a happiness magnet by adopting positivity and living your dreams today.** Happiness rules when you are with your near and dear ones. You don't have to make effort to Smile. It automatically appears on your face.

I'm sure if you keep reading, referring, sharing these thoughts and quotes, you may derive inspiration and develop a good understanding of various perspectives and facts of life. I sincerely hope, you will find this book amazing, interesting, rejuvenating, unique and constant source of inspiration.

Thank You and Happy Reading.

HAPPINESS MAGNET

© **HAPPINESS MAGNET**
BY SANDEEP RAVIDUTT SHARMA

Many of the words we speak has got more than one meaning, it's how you present them that conveys the meaning to the listener. Ensure what you intended is what got conveyed.

© HAPPINESS MAGNET
BY SANDEEP RAVIDUTT SHARMA

© **Copyright 2018 Sandeep Ravidutt Sharma - All rights reserved.**

In no way is it legal to reproduce, duplicate, or transmit any part of this document in either electronic means or in printed format. Recording of this publication is strictly prohibited and any storage of this document is not allowed unless with written permission from the publisher. All rights reserved. The information provided herein is stated to be truthful and consistent, in that any liability, in terms of inattention or otherwise, by any usage or abuse of any policies, processes, or directions contained within is the solitary and utter responsibility of the recipient reader. Under no circumstances will any legal responsibility or blame be held against the author / publisher for any reparation, damages, or monetary loss due to the information herein, either directly or indirectly. The author own all copyrights.

Legal Notice:
This book is copyright protected. This is only for personal use. You cannot amend, distribute, sell, use, quote or paraphrase any part or the content within this book without the consent of the author or copyright owner. Legal action will be pursued if this is breached.

Disclaimer Notice:
Please note the information contained within this book is for motivational, educational and knowledge sharing purpose only. Every attempt has been made to provide the reader accurate, up to date and reliable complete information. No warranties of any kind are expressed or implied. Readers acknowledge that the author is not engaging in the rendering of legal, financial, medical or professional advice. By reading this document, the reader agrees that under no circumstances the author / publisher is responsible for any losses, direct or indirect, which are incurred as a result of the use of information contained within this document, including, but not limited to, —errors, omissions, or inaccuracies.

If you have further questions, contact on
Tel: +919969256731
Email: sandeepraviduttsharma@gmail.com

© HAPPINESS MAGNET
BY SANDEEP RAVIDUTT SHARMA

Dedication

This book is dedicated to **Goddess Bhairavi**. In the Hindu religion, the Goddess Bhairavi represents divine anger and wrath which is directed towards impurities within us as well as to the negative forces that obstructs our spiritual growth. Bhairavi Mata is also called as **Shubhamkari** and does good things. She is often depicted in images as holding a book, rosary and making abhaya and varada mudra with her hands. She is fiercely protective, lending us wisdom and power, steadiness and clarity. She personifies light and fire, supporting us to reveal what we keep hidden and inviting us to explore our hidden mind and any secret darkness.

I hereby recite the following Bhairavi mool mantra...
"Om Hreem Bhairavi Kalaum Hreem Svaha"
And pray to **Goddess Bhairavi** for lending wisdom and power, steadiness and clarity in the life of my readers and the world. May Goddess Bhairavi protect us from negative forces along with removing impurities of our mind.

© **HAPPINESS MAGNET**
BY SANDEEP RAVIDUTT SHARMA

Don't wait for any external motivation whenever you are down. You know what works best for you. Self-motivation is the best way forward.

© **HAPPINESS MAGNET**
BY SANDEEP RAVIDUTT SHARMA

The world may end any day that doesn't mean we stop living and performing. The show must go on till the last second.

Freedom is precious. Remember our ancestors have earned it for us. Don't let it go.

© **HAPPINESS MAGNET**
BY SANDEEP RAVIDUTT SHARMA

Seriousness adds more value when you are attempting to change the life of the deprived for the greater good.

As you turn the pages of your life, the mystery of yesterday unfolds. A life book is full of surprises and shocks. What comes next will be known to you only when the time comes.

© HAPPINESS MAGNET
BY SANDEEP RAVIDUTT SHARMA

If you choose to travel in a train of prosperity and happiness. It will halt at your station to pick you up and take you places visualised in your dream earlier. Your choice makes you what you are.

Wishes fly out in the air when they see action on the ground.

© **HAPPINESS MAGNET**
BY SANDEEP RAVIDUTT SHARMA

Strange things happen in life for a reason.

Time follows the leader You may stop asking time when your deeds are way ahead of the current times.

Have faith in the Lord and your own capabilities. Nothing is impossible to achieve.

There is nothing wrong if you talk to strangers provided they don't act strangely.

Beautiful flowers do shy away when you smile at them.

When you entered this world, you have made a promise to the creator or God that you will spread love, kindness, compassion and happiness all around. With the passage of time, some of you have forgotten the promise and reserved these gifts for only you and some near and dear ones. It's time to honour your promise to the Lord.

Don't punish those who told lies for the greater good.

© HAPPINESS MAGNET
BY SANDEEP RAVIDUTT SHARMA

To write beautiful or ugly on a blackboard is your choice. You attract what you think.

Make amends to your lifestyle, and you can change for the good.

Doing things half-heartedly will take you nowhere. Complete involvement and your passion can only ensure the successful implementation of the planned activity.

© **HAPPINESS MAGNET**
BY SANDEEP RAVIDUTT SHARMA

Attract abundance by strongly visualising its presence already in your life.

Fortunate ones are blessed with the company of like-minded individuals who can understand and advise them better.

You may see mud or greenery, depending on what rules your mind at that point. You may also have a balanced view of both good and bad things in life.

Honour your committment and your credibility gets enhanced. Stress befriends those who over commit.

© **HAPPINESS MAGNET**
BY SANDEEP RAVIDUTT SHARMA

Thoughts rotate from one to another. Not everyone picks it up at the matching frequency. Be ready to retain the best ones and innovate.

Be selfish when it's a matter of acquiring knowledge.

You can't order Joy in your life. It's already around you, just observe tiny balloons of joy which keeps rising in the Sky of your mind from the Earth of your efforts every second.

The seeker of truth doesn't bother about false allegations and propaganda.

© **HAPPINESS MAGNET**
BY SANDEEP RAVIDUTT SHARMA

Great leaders inspire those who aspire to lead.

As you climb up the ladder of success, don't forget that between each step there is a gap which can engulf your success within minutes. So mind it, scaling each step would require complete focus, attention, energy and the right timing.

© **HAPPINESS MAGNET**
BY SANDEEP RAVIDUTT SHARMA

Choose to become somebody rather remain as nobody throughout your life.

Over the ages, the generations have changed, but the mission of humanity is the same. Live and let live.

Turn around in time to see the glowing world ready to cheer for you.

© HAPPINESS MAGNET
BY SANDEEP RAVIDUTT SHARMA

Running away from a problem would bring down your confidence level to its lowest level. Face the issues head on... Don't bother about the results. Even if you don't win, you will have the satisfaction for having tried hard.

© **HAPPINESS MAGNET**
BY SANDEEP RAVIDUTT SHARMA

If you are tired take a break but don't quit.

Help people to achieve success faster than they could do on their own. But do explain them that life is not all about success and money.

© **HAPPINESS MAGNET**
BY SANDEEP RAVIDUTT SHARMA

Transform your life by abstaining from greed and paying attention to not just your need but others as well.

Blessings keep pouring in for the kind.

© **HAPPINESS MAGNET**
BY SANDEEP RAVIDUTT SHARMA

When you share your joy with others it multiplies manifold. The opposite is the case with grief when someone shares your grief it reduces.

You may get what you want only when it remains etched on your mind and focused efforts are directed towards it.

Trust needs to be earned and not forced.

© **HAPPINESS MAGNET**
BY SANDEEP RAVIDUTT SHARMA

Rush in to rescue your good thoughts before they die. Good thoughts is the key to the door of happiness.

Your plans are good, but God's plan is grand. Be happy when things go the God's way.

Friendship blooms only when selfish behaviour is left out. Happiness rules when you are with your friends.

© **HAPPINESS MAGNET**
BY SANDEEP RAVIDUTT SHARMA

Do not sit in the Sun if you like the cool breeze coming your way that makes you happy. Take a walk on the shore and you can be happy.

The challenges in life when faced with determination ultimately become a power booster for you. Winning against the challenges makes one happy.

Behold the virtues of kindness and decent behaviour amidst chaos and turmoil. Kindness shows the path of happiness to one and all.

Turn deaf to those who like to discourage. Pay attention to those who are distributing the elixir of happiness and joyfulness.

Get away quickly if you are more likely to invite problems than resolution. Be ready to resolve and endorse happiness rather than dive into the pain and sufferings.

On the canvas of life, you can paint joy or sorrow. The choice is all yours.

© **HAPPINESS MAGNET**
BY SANDEEP RAVIDUTT SHARMA

Blessings have the power to cure anything in this world. So open up to the world with kindness, and tons of blessings will follow. Be kind to yourself and others.

The path of cruelty often leads to the door of hell. You practice kindness to convert this earth into heaven.

One should not try to act God when one has not even learned to become a complete human.

The struggle in life is never-ending. Live it but don't leave it. Maintain a positive attitude at all times and draw happiness even from your struggle.

© HAPPINESS MAGNET
BY SANDEEP RAVIDUTT SHARMA

Give due credit to the winner even when you have lost the game. Replace jealousy with happiness for the other and someday it knocks your door.

Not everyone gets what they deserve in life. Those who are fortunate should be thankful to the Lord.

Pull yourself out of your comfort zone if you intend to innovate.

God is everywhere When you read this post, God is right there with you. You don't have to even look for God if your thoughts and actions are pure. You can feel his presence in everything around you and right inside your own soul.

Run after money...but don't let money run over you.

Shed your ego if it is leading to the souring of your relationship.

Practice compassion and discipline when it's your turn to express your anguish leading to chaos.

Courage waits for you on the other side of fear, move forward with determination.

© **HAPPINESS MAGNET**
BY SANDEEP RAVIDUTT SHARMA

With each passing day you are growing old only when you start believing it that way. Feel young at heart and life will be wonderful, and you can look forward to the next day to celebrate again.

An apology is no apology if it remains inaudible to the recipient and doesn't come from the heart.

© **HAPPINESS MAGNET**
BY SANDEEP RAVIDUTT SHARMA

The beginning doesn't depend on the past. It's a way of creating everything again without any kind of influence.

Freedom is what you always craved for. When you get it, you will have to be more responsible.

© **HAPPINESS MAGNET**
BY SANDEEP RAVIDUTT SHARMA

One drop of happiness is good enough to convert Ocean of sorrow.

You get inspired automatically only when you are ready to receive.

Digest all sorrows with the hope that next time happiness will be served.

Your good karma in life can still make you a stone in your next life, but it would be divine if God's idol is carved out of it.

Your heart is programmed by the creator to see the best and beautiful things and beings in life.

© HAPPINESS MAGNET
BY SANDEEP RAVIDUTT SHARMA

Open the window of your mind and let the glow of positivity enter your thoughts and heart.

The world looks at you with attention only when you have gained confidence and declared your intention to perform on the global stage.

© **HAPPINESS MAGNET**
BY SANDEEP RAVIDUTT SHARMA

The caravan of Golden happiness is coming towards you. Get ready at your door to greet cheerfully and embrace it wholeheartedly.

You can shower wealth only if you have. But kindness can be showered without the limitations.

Cheer the Challenger, and you are likely to uncover the new winner.

© **HAPPINESS MAGNET**
BY SANDEEP RAVIDUTT SHARMA

Life behaves strangely every minute. When the response is favourable, you feel happy and in adverse times you blame it all on life. Remember life appears the way you have carved it on your own. So stop complaining instead act in time.

Believe in your own self and the world will believe you. Smile and see the world smiles back at you.

Be kind to yourself if you can do this then you can be kind to others as well.

Silence is Golden when chaos rules in the neighbourhood.

The sky changes its outlook every now and then. Change is the only constant in this beautiful world. Embrace the change without any hesitation and with high hopes for the greater good.

Those who took the escalator route at the start of their career often find its hard to climb the stairs if they were pushed to the bottom again.

Wrong choices ensure failure. Failure, in turn, challenges you. If you accept them and take a vow not to repeat the same mistakes again, success can be all yours.

© **HAPPINESS MAGNET**
BY SANDEEP RAVIDUTT SHARMA

Once words are fired, there is no way you can bring them back. Always choose your words well before you speak.

Update yourself if you want to stay relevant with the fast changing world.

The future appears to blur if you are hardly focusing on your karma in the present.

Time changes your position in life. Sometimes the stick is in your hand, and you make the world run. In contrast, a time comes when you need the stick to take the next step forward gently.

As you walk with the intent to find your way to your destination. You will notice that as you take the next step the immediate path will appear clear and the rest still appears to blur. To win, you need to take one step at a time. If the next step is clear to you then don't bother about what lies ahead. Focus on now...meaning your current step. Gradually you will reach your goal post.

Don't wait for others to tell you that you are beautiful. Believe in your self that you are the finest creation of this Universe.

Time plays the flute for you and can be brute as well.

Those who seek knowledge find it even in their empty hands. Those who are not bothered to gain knowledge don't know its worth even if they have their hands full of it.

At times you have got the winning edge but still, you may lose mainly due to the passionate and more intelligent opponent who performed better than you.

Get inspiration from the waves. Waves travel again and again just to touch the shore. Keep Going is the mantra of success.

You are incomparable with anyone. You are born with unique talent and characteristics. You are here to stay and win.

You know more than what is being taught to you by your Gurus. All you have to do is explore your inner self and soul.

It's your timely efforts of today that decides whether you will fast or feast tomorrow.

© **HAPPINESS MAGNET**
BY SANDEEP RAVIDUTT SHARMA

Your health is in your hands. Identify the right point to heal the pain of your life. Work enough to replace the frown with a smile.

Childhood is the best gift of the creator to mankind. Never let the innocence and joyfulness of your childhood vanish when you grow up in life.

Time doesn't wait for you even for a second. Be ready to rise and reach early to remain in total control of your schedule of task for the day.

You gain or lose not because of your own performance but also due to extra and excellence effort put in by your opponent.

Success is always one step ahead of the failure. The day you learn how to bridge the gap you achieve success.

You can't change the way people look at you, but can very well change the way you look at them.

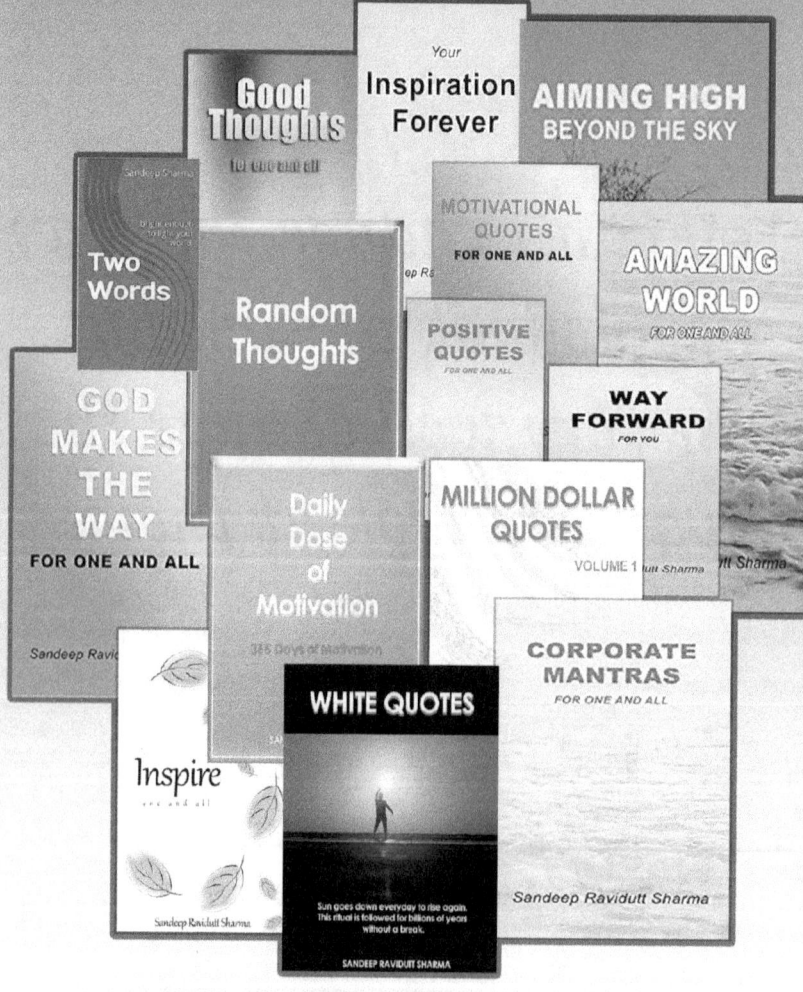

www.ingramcontent.com/pod-product-compliance
Lightning Source LLC
Chambersburg PA
CBHW070803220526
45466CB00002B/523